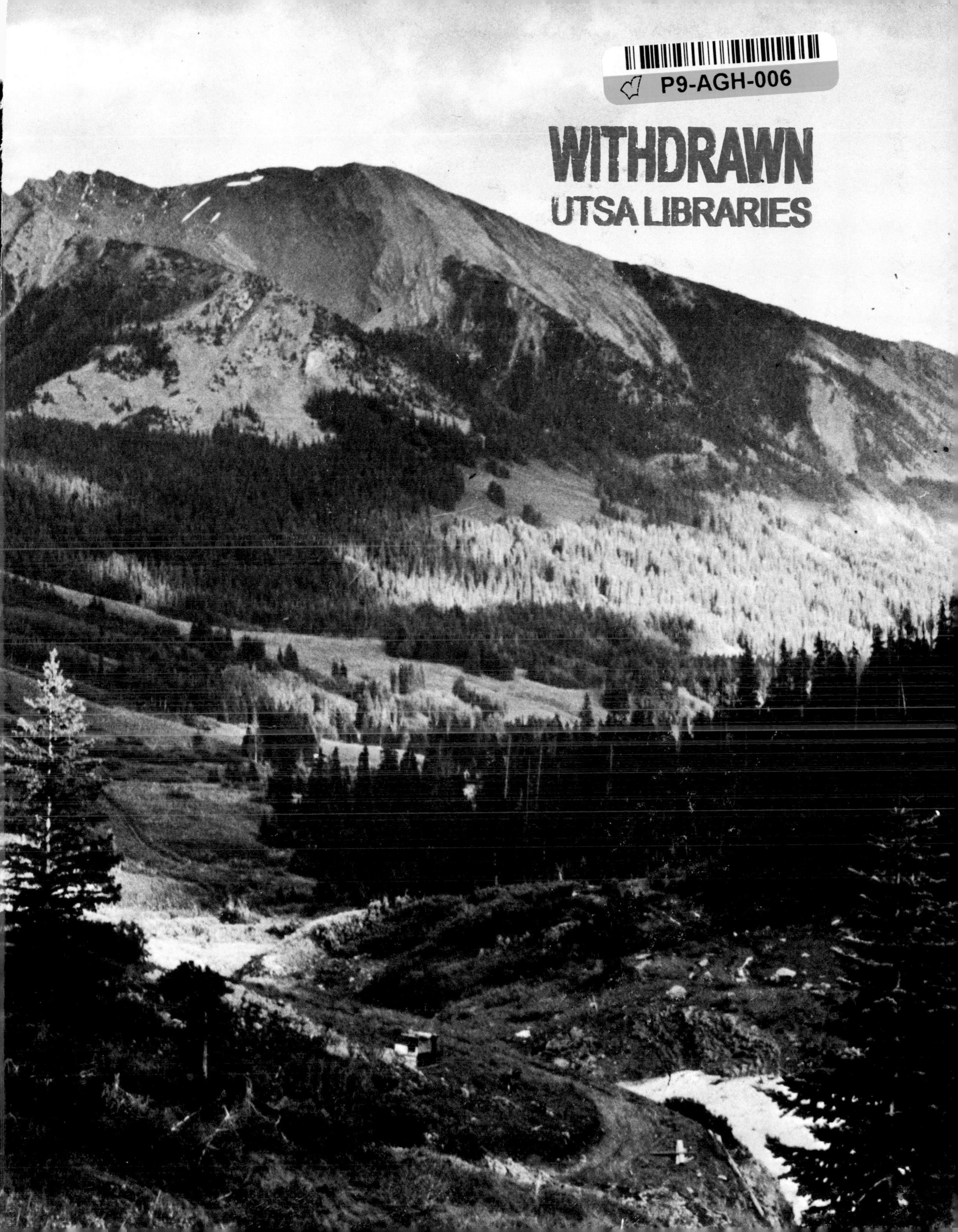

PHOTOGRAPHS OF AMERICAN NATURE

EDWIN WAY TEALE

PHOTOGRAPHS OF AMERICAN NATURE

Dodd, Mead & Company
New York

Edwin Way Teale, whose work has been recognized by the Burroughs Medal and the Pulitzer Prize, is also the author of *Grassroot Jungles, The Golden Throng, Near Horizons, Dune Boy, The Lost Woods, Days Without Time, Circle of the Seasons, Adventures in Nature, The Strange Lives of Familiar Insects, Springtime in Britain,* and the four-volume work *The American Seasons,* comprising *North With the Spring, Journey Into Summer, Autumn Across America,* and *Wandering Through Winter.* He has illustrated and added commentary to an edition of Thoreau's *Walden* and has compiled *The Insect World of J. Henri Fabre, The Wilderness World of John Muir,* and *The Thoughts of Thoreau.*

ISBN: 0-396-06713-1
Library of Congress Catalog Card Number: 72-5876
Printed in the United States of America

Designed by Sidney Feinberg

Foreword

For all who love the out-of-doors, special dawns and twilights, glimpses into the worlds of wild creatures, the slant of light among trees, the glint of sunshine on water, natural beauties in a thousand forms haunt the memory. But the sharpness of these mental pictures usually diminishes; their images become less clear; imperceptibly they fade away. When, in some fortunate split second of time, a camera catches on film the mood, the action, the life, and the beauty of some outstanding moment, it contributes a kind of permanence of its own to a memory. At a glance and after the passage of years, it has the power to evoke the atmosphere, the emotions, the sense of wonder that characterized that instant of the past.

The urge to capture and store away these crystallized memories is a passion that adds a particular delight and satisfaction to the life of the photographer of the out-of-doors. His pictures preserve, with the vividness of a first-hand encounter, his past experiences in nature. Through them, repeatedly and at length, he can savor his former enjoyments.

Photographs of nature may be many things. Some may be primarily artistic; some may be primarily scientific. In their simplest, most matter-of-fact form, they are merely "catalogue" pictures of objects or creatures. The best in nature photography, however, records both the object and its setting. It arrests, in its normal surroundings, some form of life, portraying it in a characteristic moment of its existence. Such pictures possess emotional as well as intellectual impact. This is accomplished without trickery or distortion. Nature is recorded faithfully. But in addition to delineating sharply the central subject, there is captured its special niche in nature, the small individual world which it inhabits. Such photographs carry us on an adventure of discovery. They let us enter into nature's diversification of habitats—the seashore, the mossy forest, the pond edge, the desert, the jungle of the grassblades.

Two interacting skills, like two hands, aid the art of the nature photographer. One is his technical knowledge of photography, his familiarity with cameras, lenses, films, and lighting. The other, no less important, is his understanding of nature. The more he knows of the habits of wild creatures, the times of day when certain events take place, the blooming dates of flowers, the psychology of particular animals, the greater his chances of success. His photographic equipment is important. But it is often less elaborate equipment than a wide knowledge of nature, an eye for lighting and angle of view and composition of picture, that accounts for the outstanding nature photograph.

As an aid to observing and photographing small creatures in their natural surroundings, for a decade and a half I rented the "insect rights" to an old orchard hillside on the south shore of Long Island. There I set out bushes and plants to attract various six-legged creatures within reach of my lens and my magnifying glass. Some of the thousands of pictures that resulted illustrated two of my early books, *Grassroot Jungles* and *Near Horizons*. Later, in gathering material for four books on the American seasons, I found fresh fields for nature photography wherever I went: in the Florida Everglades, in the Colorado Rockies, in the Arizona desert, on the Great Plains, among the tidepools of the Northwest. Selections from this harvest of pictures have been hung in the salon of the Royal Photographic Society of Great Britain and have appeared in one-man shows and traveling exhibitions in museums throughout America. Over a period of forty years, I have added to a file of nature pictures that now includes more than twenty-five thousand negatives.

In going over these thousands of negatives as I made the final selection of pictures for this book, I found the hours filled with vivid recollections. I recalled changing film on a floating island in Florida; hunching motionless among biting blackflies waiting for a little Kirtland's warbler to return to its nest in the jack pines of Michigan; wandering for hours across the high flower fields above the timberline in the Rockies. I remembered how the picture of the snowy owl, number 160, nearly resulted in the loss of my left eye. This visitor from the far north had been found with an injured wing on Long Island and I had taken it to the Tackapausha Museum, at Seaford. Later, when its wing mended and the owl was ready to be released, I took the picture shown in this volume. Hardly had I snapped the shutter when it launched out, flew low above my head, and as it passed by lowered one foot and raked

my cheek with its needle-sharp claws. They left three cuts half an inch below my eye.

Among these returning memories, probably the strangest was that of a morning on the shore of Lake Michigan in the Indiana dunes. The day before, the Fourth of July, the beach had been trampled by innumerable visitors. During the night slow waves had pushed their water up among the depressions in the sand. It had swirled this way and that and had left behind the forms of various creatures, as shown in picture number 199. That strange, dreamlike experience is one that has never been repeated.

It is a far cry from the wet plates of the earliest nature photographers to the compact cameras, the high-speed film, the electronic flash of today. Innumerable technological advances—particularly the flash—have aided the work of the outdoors cameraman. The first pictures I ever took with an electronic flash recorded the images of the baby cottontails—first three, then two, then one. Sometime during the 1940s, I had stopped to see my friend Henry B. Kane, the artist-photographer whose illustrations added to the attractiveness of so many nature volumes. As Alumni Secretary of the Massachusetts Institute of Technology, he was well acquainted with the inventor of the stroboscopic light, Dr. Harold E. Edgerton. He had brought one of the experimental models home to Lincoln, Massachusetts. While I was there, his son, David, discovered a nest of baby cottontails. We rounded up three. Before they could explode into action, I focused on them, opened the shutter, and Henry Kane tripped the split-second stab of light. One little rabbit dashed away. We repeated the process with two baby rabbits. Another bolted off and, in a final picture, we photographed the remaining one.

Of the 289 pictures contained in this book, nearly half a hundred are published here for the first time. In arrangement, the sequence of the photographs carries the reader up the Atlantic Coast from Florida to Maine, then westward across the country—as the pioneers advanced—to end in the far Northwest on the Pacific Coast.

During the years these pictures of American nature have been recorded, many things have altered. Celilo Falls, where Indians took their annual harvest of salmon long before the Lewis and Clark Expedition, has disappeared beneath the water impounded behind a Columbia River dam. The beautiful Burgaw Savanna of the Cape Fear region of North Carolina, where insectivorous plants once flourished in wild abundance, has been obliterated to make way for blueberry fields. The dune country of northern Indiana is scarred and altered. My Insect Garden, which once attracted strange and beautiful creatures, long since became an extension of a schoolyard. In the West, over large areas, the prairie dog has been poisoned out of existence and, in the East, the duck hawk is at present virtually unknown, a victim of DDT.

More than a century ago, in eastern Massachusetts, Henry Thoreau complained that he could find only a mutilated copy of the complete poem of nature. Whole pages had been torn out by the activity of his ancestors who had laid waste the woods and wildlife he wished to enjoy. During all the intervening years this process of destruction has continued at an accelerated pace. How much, except for the click of a shutter in years past, would be lost to all but individual memory!

The three baby cottontails, the coot feeding in its circle of ripples, the luna moth hanging in all its soft beauty waiting for the coming of night—all these as individuals disappeared years ago. But in their photographs they live on. In this present time of swift and widespread change it is fortunate that never before have so many cameras been recording so much, that photography is amassing a pictorial record of the land and its inhabitants unparalleled in the past.

EDWIN WAY TEALE

Trail Wood,
Hampton, Connecticut
May 1, 1972.

Sequence of Photographs

1. American coot feeding among leaves of spatterdock, the yellow pond lily, in the Everglades.

3. Ring-billed gull hovering above a beach on the Gulf Coast of Florida.

2. Spatterdock leaves massed together on the surface of the water in a southern swamp.

4. Great white heron by a drainage ditch. The entire range of this bird is confined to lower Florida.

5. The author, on a Florida beach, surrounded by a flock of ring-billed gulls.

6. Sandy Key at the lower end of Florida Bay. Here John James Audubon studied birds in 1832.

7. Indigo snake attacking a diamondback. Pictures 8–13 show steps in its victorious battle.

14. Spanish moss growing on a live oak on Bull's Island, off the South Carolina Coast.

15. Following two pages: Shadbush in bloom in the Great Smoky Mountains of Tennessee.

Insectivorous plants of a southern savanna. 16. Pitcher plant, top, left and, 17, butterwort, right.
Below, 18, sundew, left and, 19, Venus's-flytrap, right.

20. Clapper rail nesting among swirling *Spartina* grass on a Long Island sea meadow.

21. King, or horseshoe, crabs coming from the sea to spawn. Above: 22. Massed in shallows, top, left and, 23, burrowing in mud. Below: 24. Wandering over sand flats and, 25, left stranded at ebb-tide.

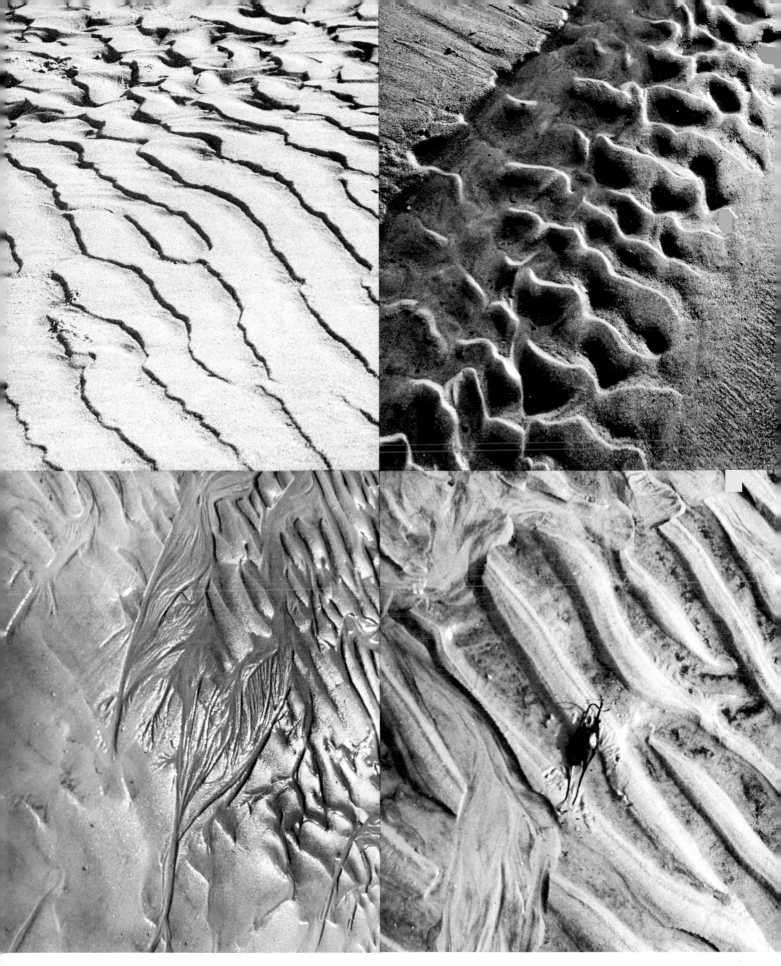

26-34. Varied forms of ripple marks left exposed at the sea's edge by the ebbing of the tide.

35. Mottled coloring camouflages the eggs in the nest of a plover on the sand of a sea beach.

36. Eelgrass, the chief food of the brant, twines thickly in shallow bays along the Atlantic Coast.

37. The sunset shore. Opposite page, 38–41, scenes at the edge of the sea.

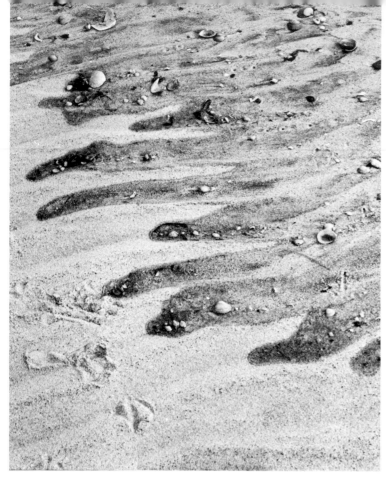

42. High tide on rippled sand.

43. Channels cut in mud.

44. Sand dollar.

45. Spiny urchin.

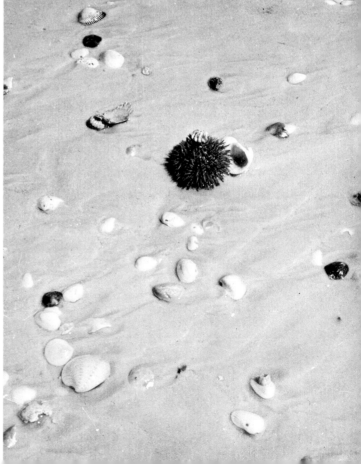

46. As the water recedes behind it, a dead skate lies stranded at the edge of the Cape Cod shore.

47. Sunset over Crocker Lake, near the Canadian boundary above Moose River in northern Maine.

48. Gnarled roots of a yellow birch cascade over rocks to reach the earth in an Adirondack forest.

49. Rays of the rising sun stream through early autumn mist among the forest trees near Crocker Lake in northern Maine.

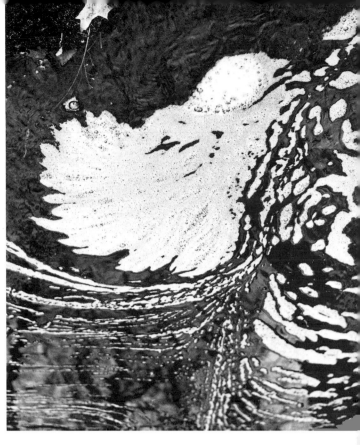

51. Fungus on a tree trunk.

52. Foam on a New England brook.

53. Witch hazel leaves.

54. Lady ferns.

50. A young raccoon finds a lookout in the crotch of a wild cherry tree.

56. The shore line of Walden as it curves away from the eastern end of the pond.

55. Five baby screech owls just emerged from their nest in an old linden tree.

59. Fairhaven Bay on the Sudbury River and, 60, Deep Cove on the north shore of Walden Pond.

57. Pickerelweed beside the Concord River and, 58, the town of Concord seen from the road to Walden Pond.

61. View of Walden Pond looking from the north shore not far from where, in 1845, Henry Thoreau built his hut a mile and a half from Concord.

63. Whitefooted mouse at the entrance of its winter home, a bluebird nesting box in New England.

62. Ripple rings on the water of Deep Cove on a misty morning in September.

64. Marsh marigold.

65. Painted trillium.

66. Pink lady's-slipper.

67. Violets.

68. The rare and colorful showy lady's-slipper.

69. The massed white flowers of the bloodroot.

70. Clouds and sunset
behind a wild cherry tree
at the edge of a Long Island
sea meadow.

72. Blacksnake in search of prey winding among the plants of a rock garden.

71. Mute swans nesting. While the female incubates the eggs the male parades on guard.

73. Face of the duck hawk, or peregrine falcon, prized during centuries of falconry.

74. In the early spring, a lowland stream on Long Island is bordered by lush skunk cabbage.

75. One of the year's first blooms is the flower of the skunk cabbage in its cowl-like spathe.

76. A young salamander, the red eft or newt, creeping through moss at the edge of a woodland stream.

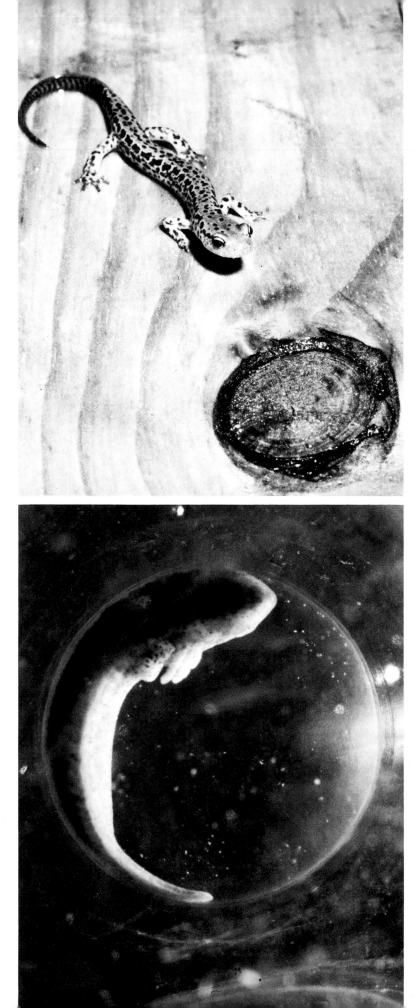

77. Long-tailed salamander from Audubon's Pennsylvania home and, below, 78, salamander in egg.

79. Closeup of toad, top right. 80. Gray tree frog calling, near right. 81. The spring peeper, far right.

82. In a small pond in the Hudson River Valley a bullfrog suns itself on a floating log.

83. Young robins being fed at a nest secreted in the interior of a pine tree.

84. Baby phoebes
overflowing their nest.

85. A pair of mallards
with their ducklings.

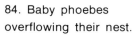

86. A parent flicker
with a young bird looking
from its nesting hole in
an old apple tree

87. Three baby rabbits.
88. Two baby rabbits.
89. One baby rabbit.
Young cottontails just
out of the nest.

91. Broad-leaved grass at the garden, top left and, 92, morning-glories. Below, 93, mist and, 94, snow.

90. The Insect Garden in the spring with apple trees in bloom.

95. Painting bumblebees with colored spots to identify individuals for study at the Insect Garden.

96. Praying mantis reared up on an Insect Garden plant awaiting the approach of its prey.

After mating, the female mantis often consumes her mate. These three pictures, 97–99, show the sequence of the feast.

100. Mantis making its last molt and becoming a winged adult.

101. A female mantis depositing hundreds of eggs in a mass of froth that hardens into a protecting case.

103. A fly with its legs imprisoned in slits on a milkweed flower. Larger insects escape carrying pollen.

104. May beetle with antennae expanded like moosehorns and, 105, climbing among tangled grass blades.

106. A carpenter ant gathering honeydew from treehopper nymphs on a sunflower leaf.

107. Grasshopper balanced on the slender stem of a grass clump.

108. A seventeen-year cicada emerging from its nymphal shell.

109. The predaceous bug *Podisus* holding a captured tent caterpillar with its unfolded sucking beak.

111. A curled-over iris leaf provides shelter for the night for a *Chlorion* digger wasp.

110. A damselfly, with many-veined wings, seen in silhouette clinging to the bud of a tiger lily.

112. In the sunshine a dragonfly clings to a leaf of sweet flag encircled by bindweed.

113. A ladybird beetle climbing over the purple flower-head of a large thistle.

114. Female grasshopper with her long ovipositor, for placing eggs, extending to the rear.

115. A lacewing fly on wild lettuce. Both as a larva and an adult this insect feeds on aphids.

118. Carolina locust on mullein lea
and below, 119, facelike markings or
a saddleback caterpillar

116. A cecropia moth and below,
117, the false eye-spots on the larva
of the spicebush swallowtail.

120. Cranefly clinging with its long, slender legs to grass that has gone to seed.

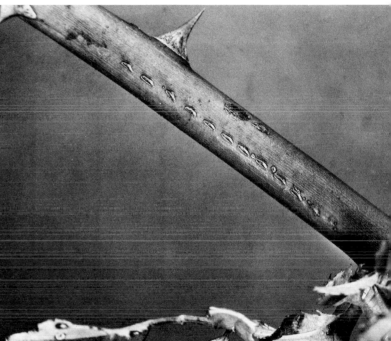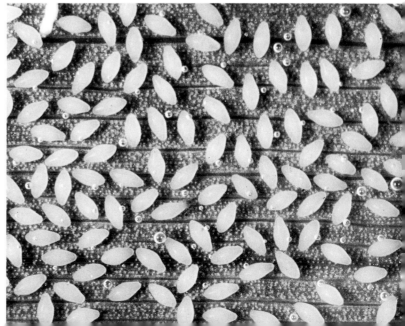

138. A daddy longlegs searching for food as it clambers among the blooms of a funkia plant.

137. Grasshopper ovipositor holding an egg at the tip shown opposite at lower right.

140. Dewdrops sparkle on the orb web of a garden spider after a night of early autumn mist.

139. A golden garden spider clinging to the orb web in which it catches its prey.

145. On stems of goldenrod, nests of foam protect immature froghoppers from sun and enemies.

141. Sphinx moth larva with parasite cocoons and, 142-144, the adult winged parasites emerging.

146–148. Following page: Froghoppers producing foam bubbles. 149. Nymphal skin left when adult emerges.

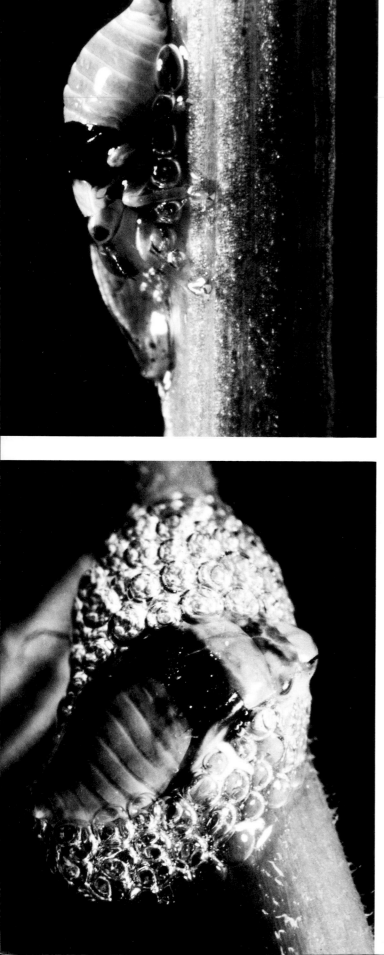
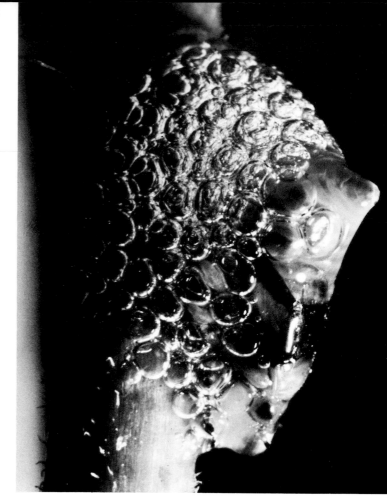

154. Midwinter snow, glazed with ice, mounded over rocks beside a small New England stream.

150. Dew on grass leaves, top left, previous page. 151. Autumn ice. 152. Lower left, frost on ivy. 153. Fallen leaves.

155. Fernlike frost decorates a windowpane after a sub-zero night in January.

157. A merganser duck resting on ice.

156. Wind-driven snow covering trees at the edge of a New England woods; the end of a blizzard.

158. Serpentine lines running along an ice-covered brook.

159. Tracks of whitefooted mice lace the snow between clumps of prostrate juniper.

160. A snowy owl driven south by scarcity of its winter food in the far north

161. Wheel of winter stars, Polaris or the north star at center, recorded on a December night.

162. Midsummer haze hangs over the Kankakee River as it winds through lowland in northern Indiana.

163. Clear Creek
in central Indiana.

164. A yellow perch
beside a sunken log.

165. Bumblebee on red clover. The long tongues of these bees transfer pollen from bloom to bloom.

167. Within the hive, the honeybees fill the six-sided waxen cells with stores of honey.

166. Honeybees obtaining apple blossom nectar which they will transform into honey.

168. Nurse bees, left, among brood cells feeding the grubs that will mature into adult workers. 169. Queen bee, above, surrounded by her court and below, 170, the strong, lightweight comb made of wax.

172. Goldenrod pollen packed into pollen baskets on the rear legs of a worker honeybee.

171. Worker bee ventilating the hive on a summer day by fanning its wings at the entrance.

173. Honeybee swarm, following page, and, 174, bees massed together in a winter cluster in the hive.

175. Polyphemus on ferns with following pictures, 176–180, showing emerged moth unfolding its wings.

181. Print visible through the transparent eye-spot on the wing of a Polyphemus moth.

182. Flowing, wind-formed hills of sand and below, 183, slanting lines of sunshine in the Indiana dunes.

184. Buried trees uncovered by movement of the dunes.

185. Circles made by grass tips.

186. Dog tracks in the dunes followed by, 187–198, the tracks of man, crow, skunk, centipede, mouse, small rodent, horned lark, beetle, muskrat, burrowing beetle, small mammal, crow and spider.

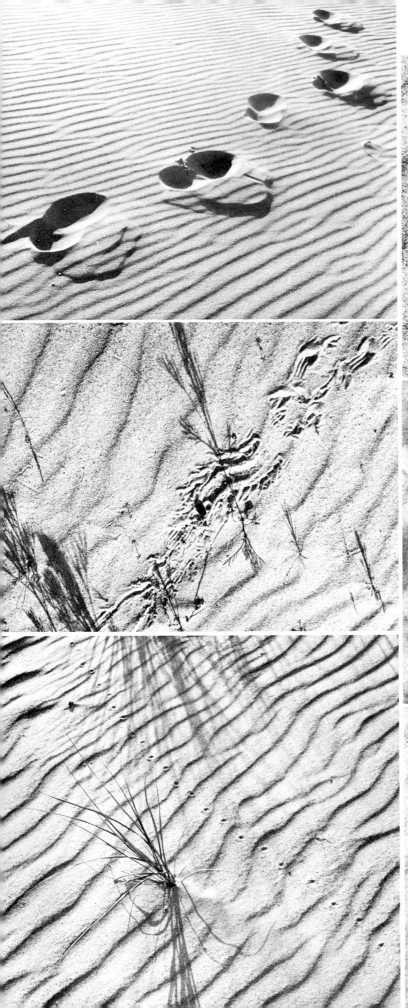
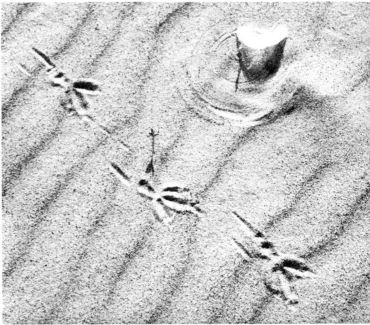
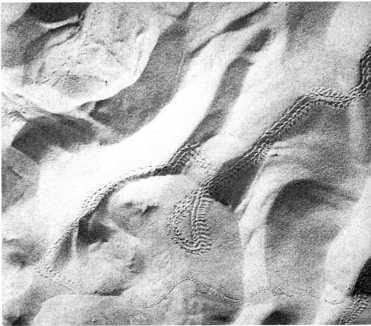

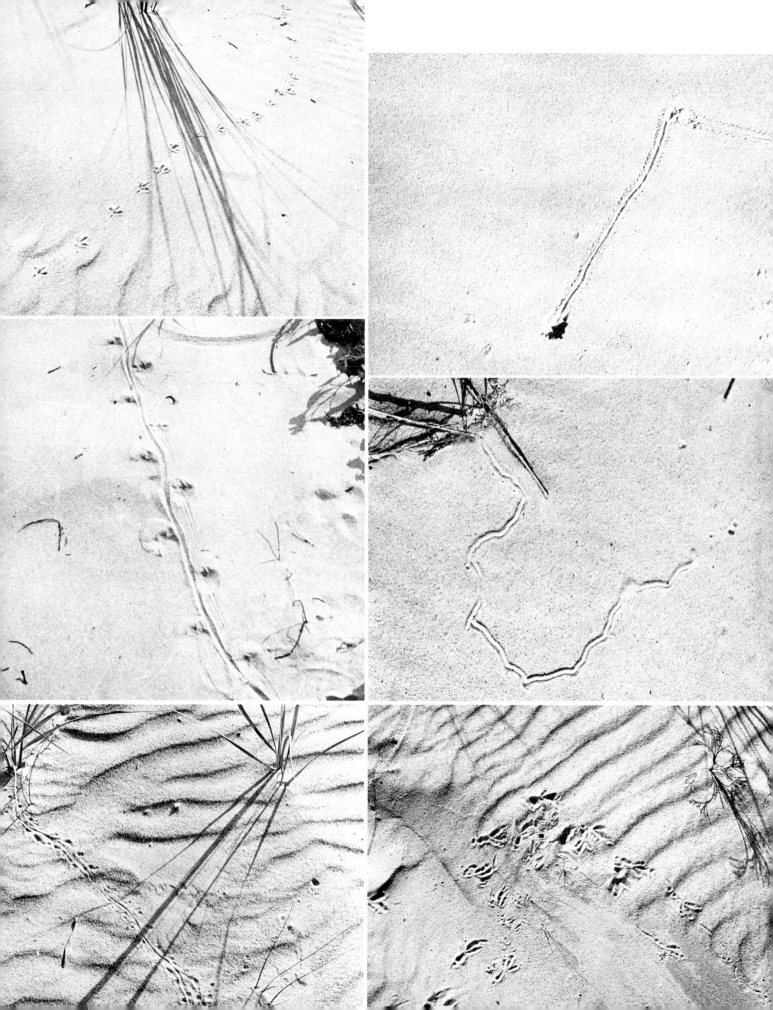

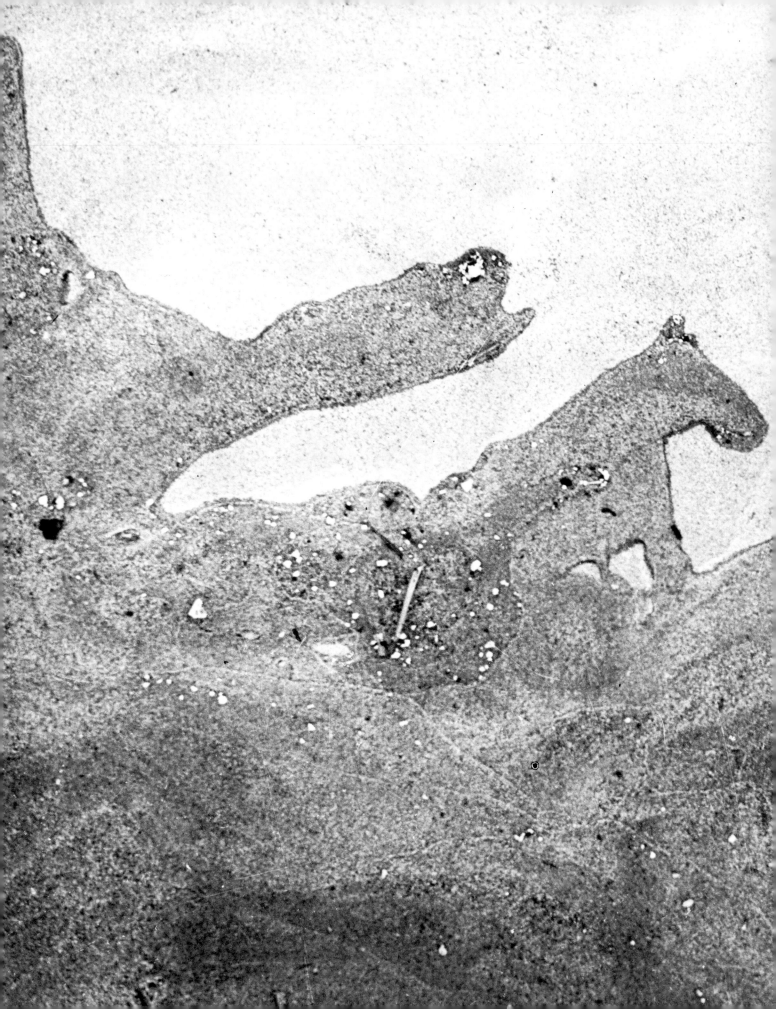

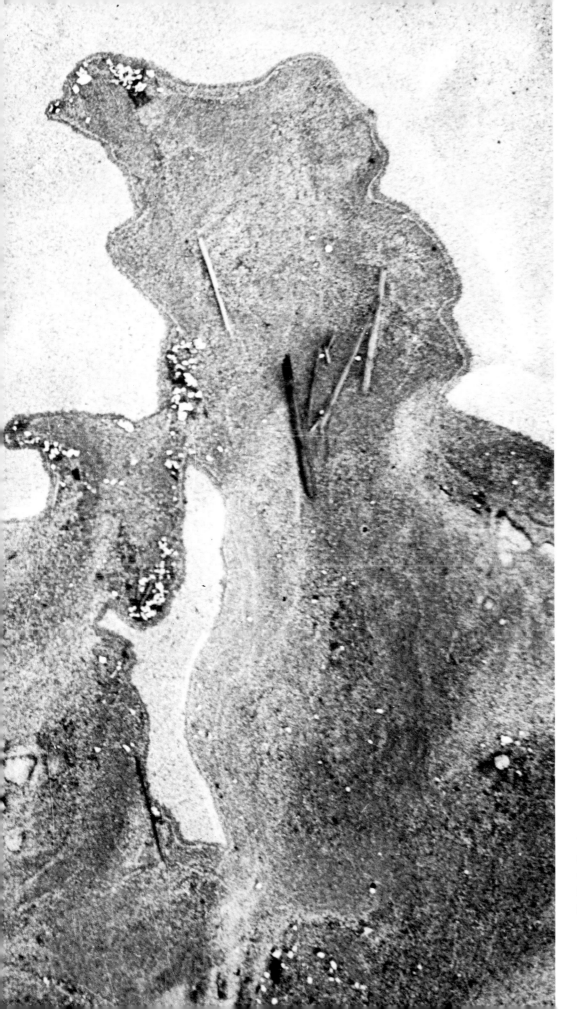

199. Forms of various creatures left by the waves of Lake Michigan on the trampled sand of the beach in the Indiana dunes.

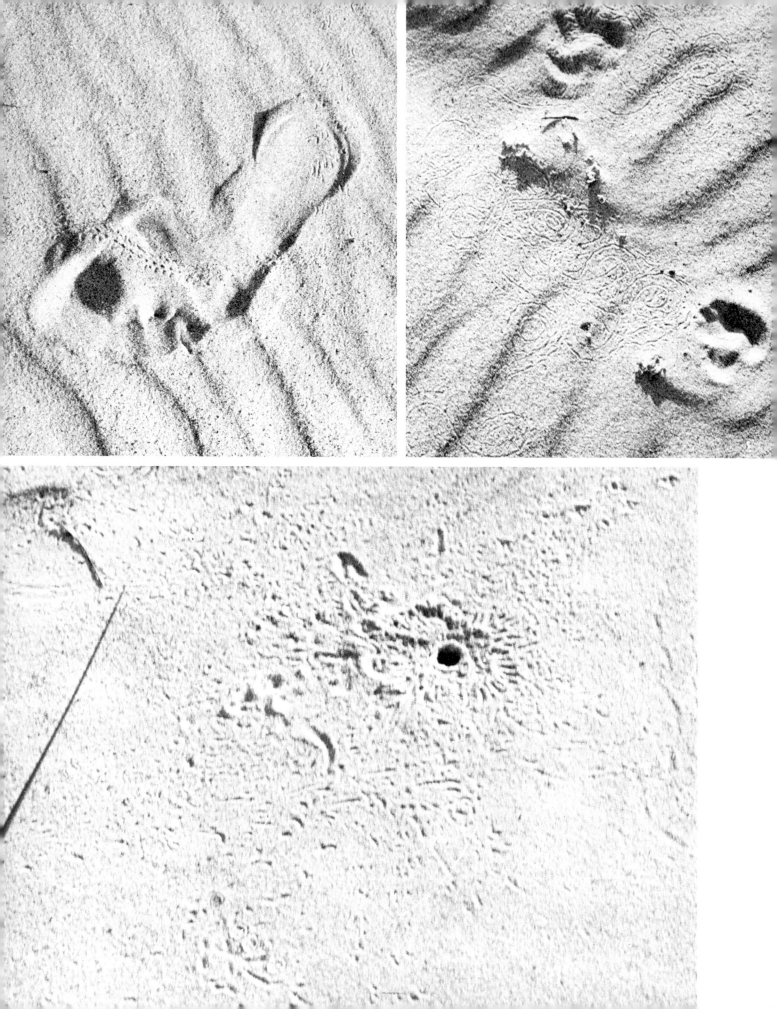

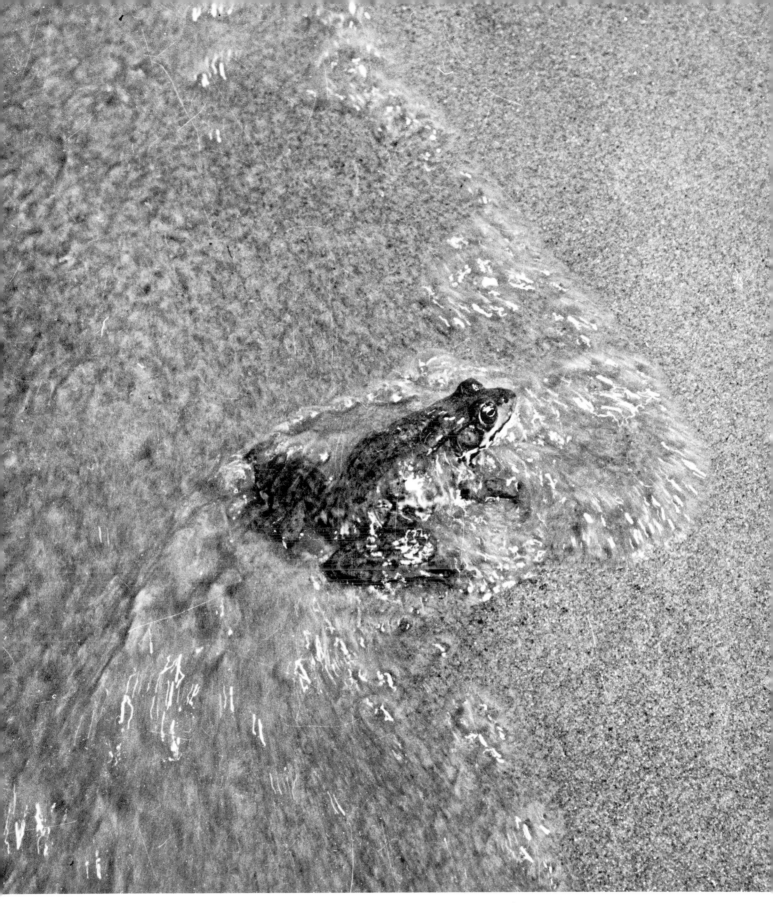

203. Frog on shore.

200–202. Tracks of man, dog, beetle, and spider on sand.

Following page, 204, luna moth.

Opposite page: 206. Newly emerged black swallowtail butterfly clinging among the flowers of narcissus. Above: 207. A monarch, or milkweed, butterfly on a mallow. Each year this insect migrates south in autumn.

Preceding page: 205. The large American silk moth, the Cecropia, waiting for dusk to become active.

210. Colorado potato beetle nibbling along the edge of a leaf on a potato plant.

208. Monarch larva on milkweed, top left, and below, 209, a monarch chrysalis attached to a milkweed leaf.

211. Robber fly, which overtakes and captures insect prey in the air, clinging to a rose petal.

214. Golden eagle screaming. In early falconry in Europe, such eagles were flown only by kings.

213. Young screech owl resting in an opening in the hollow trunk of an old apple tree.

215. Red squirrel on white birch.

216-219. Red squirrel recorded in action at a forest cabin in Maine.

220. An ear of yellow corn provides a feast for a whitefooted mouse.

221. Sunflower being examined by author.

222–225. Sunflower unfolding and, 226–229, flower to seed.

230. The rare Kirtland's warbler, breeding only in the jack pines of lower central Michigan.

231. Face of robber fly.

232. Face of hornet.

233. Face of damselfly.

236. Face of cricket.

237. Face of giant water bug.

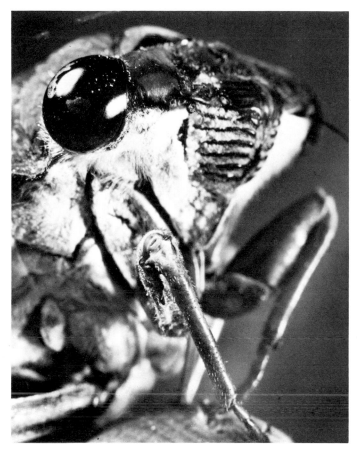

234. Face of locust.

235. Face of cicada.

238. Face of scorpion fly.

239. Face of horsefly.

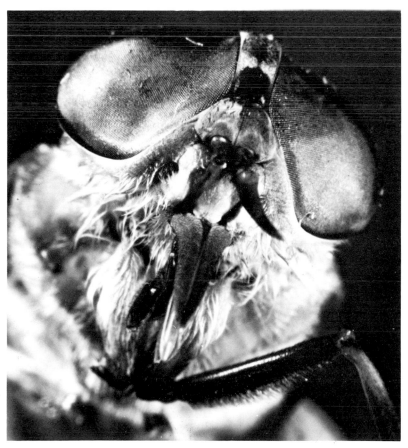

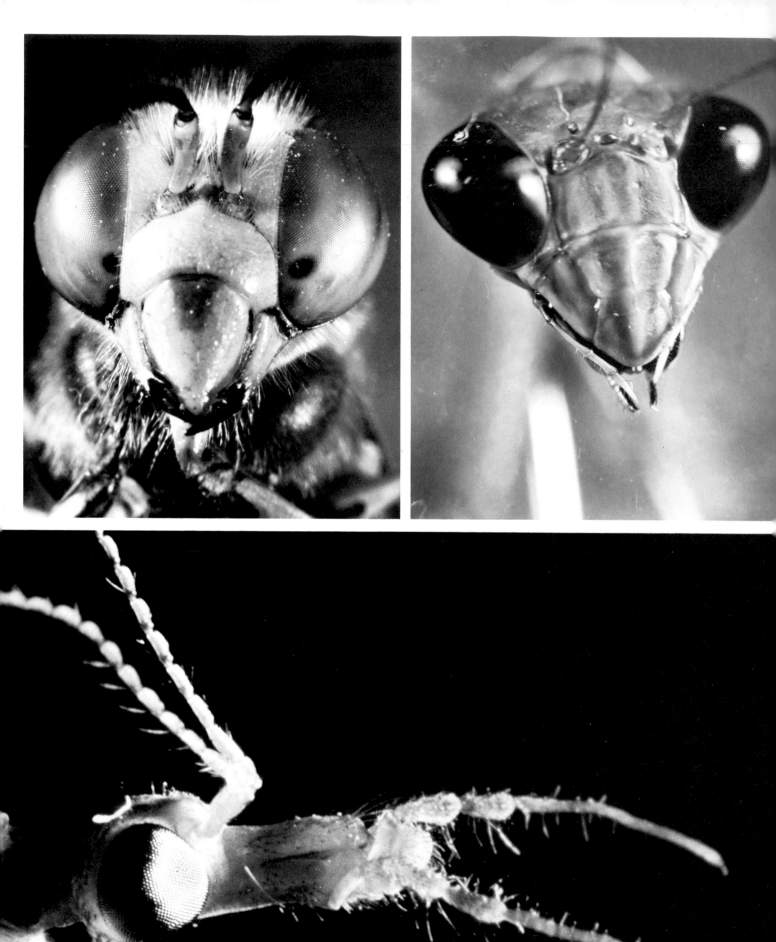

243. Fawn of a white-tailed deer photographed among cedars on the Door Peninsula of Wisconsin.

240–242. Face of digger wasp, praying mantis, lacewing fly.

244. A summer thunderhead piling up in the sky over a wheat field in the midwest.

245. Prairie dogs at Devil's Tower.

248–249. Trees of the timberline shaped by gales among the high peaks of the Colorado Rockies.

246–247. Prairie dogs and their burrows.

251. Alpine goldflower, top left and, 252, bistort; 253, lower left, queen's crown; 254, rocks on tundra.
250. Mountain meadows in bloom above the timberline near Trail Ridge Road in the Colorado Rockies.

255. A forest of saguaro cacti extends for miles across the Sonoran Desert in southern Arizona.

256. Broken trunk of saguaro, top left and, 257, saguaro with twisted branches. Lower left, 258, ring of bracing rods in trunk and, 259, new branches on trunk.

260. White pelican resting in the shallows at the edge of Aransas Bay on the coast of Texas.

263. Spiny cholla cactus shines in the backlighting of the desert sunset.

261. Rabbitbrush in the Big Bend of Texas, top left and, 262, below, ripples at White Sands.

264. A mule deer feeding in winter near the rim of the Grand Canyon in northern Arizona.

265. Aspens clad in their yellow autumn foliage mottle the slopes of the Uinta Mountains of Utah.

266. Indians with dip nets catching salmon as they leap up the Celilo Falls in the Columbia River when they return from the sea in autumn to spawn in the shallow pools of the upper stream.

267. Dead trees lie at the edge of a hot pool in the Yellowstone National Park in Wyoming.

268. Hot spring steam, top left, and, 269, sea figs. 270. Craters of the Moon and, 271, rain forest.

274. Stream flowing down from the melting front of Mt. Rainier's Nisqually Glacier.

272. Devil's Cornfield in Death Valley and below, 273, desert scene in southern California.

276. Clark's nutcracker, a bird of the northwestern mountains and forests, high on Mt. Rainier.

275. Snow-covered spires of slender spruces in the Mt. Rainier country of Washington.

277. Mt. Rainier in winter. From it flow twenty-eight glaciers, more of these rivers of ice than are produced by any other mountain in America.

On the two preceding pages:
278. Wind-shaped Monterey
cypress on the California
coast, left, and below, 279,
a Joshua tree of the desert.
280. Streamlined huckleberry
bushes on an Oregon headland
and below, 281, Darlingtonia
pitcher plants.

282. Tumbling surf shattering
against the rock of headlands
at the edge of the Pacific
on the coast of Oregon.

284. Sea lions basking beside the surf and below, 285, mossy logs in the Olympic Peninsula forest.

283. Sea lions at home in Sea Lion Cave, hollowed out by the surf at the base of an Oregon headland.

286. In the Olympic rain forest, following page, sunshine streams downward through the misty air.